GORILLAS
THE GENTLE GIANTS

Gorillas, the Gentle Giants

First published in the United Kingdom by

Evans Mitchell Books

The Old Forge

Forge Mews

16 Church Street

Rickmansworth

Hertfordshire WD3 1DH

United Kingdom

Photography copyright © 2008: Martin Harvey
except illustration and photography:
- page 98: G. Mützel (1883)
- page 105: Alain Pons
- page 15: copyright King Kong 1933 Aries/RKO
- pages 4, 22 (left), 34 & 35, 38, 39, 67 (bottom),
  71 (bottom), 79, 80 & 81, 89, 100 & 101: Cyril Ruoso
- page 54 (bottom): Bob Campbell
- page 99: Rainbow by King/Monkey Jungles,
  courtesy of Dr Anne Zeller
- page 102: Ian Redmond
- page 126: Gorilla Run, courtesy of the Gorilla
  Organization

Text copyright © 2008: Letitia Farris-Toussaint

Graphic design: Empreinte & Territoires, Paris, France
Pre-press: Studio Goustard, Vanves, France

Scientific consulting: Ian Redmond, OBE
Editing: Peter and Gillian Varley

British Library Cataloguing in Publication Data
A CIP record of this book is available on request
from the British Library.

ISBN: 978-1-901268-35-5

Printed in Italy

GORILLAS
THE GENTLE GIANTS
MARTIN HARVEY & LETITIA FARRIS-TOUSSAINT

Evans Mitchell Books

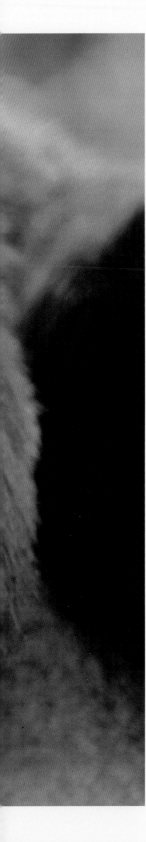

CONTENTS

INTRODUCTION

Chest-beating, tree-throwing, bull-charging, canine-baring, lion-roaring, fierce-glaring, harem-hoarding, human-looking: thus were the gorillas described by the first Europeans to bring back tales from deepest, darkest Africa. From the time the ape was first discovered in the 1800s, the gorilla had people reeling with fright and delight. Both man and beast, it was as if the gorilla had stepped right out of fairytales. Artists soon gave a new twist to *Beauty and the Beast*, portraying the silverback as an abductor of swooning, scantily-clad women. Emmanuel Frémiet's famous sculpture *Gorille enlevant une femme* even won a medal of honour at the prestigious

Paris Art Salon in 1887. But it was Merian C. Cooper's 1933 film *King Kong* starring Fay Wray that immortalized the image of the gorilla as a mighty, ferocious beast. The long list of sequels, spin-offs and remakes, the last released in 2005, attests to the gorilla's lasting grip on us – if not on Fay Wray. Unlike the earlier representations, *King Kong* nevertheless planted a seed of truth, one that would grow and eventually change our view for the better: the giant was formidable, but he was also gentle. "T'was beauty killed the beast," ends the film. Perhaps beauty has also helped to save it thus far. First, beauty in a figurative sense. Whereas the chimpanzee has often been viewed as a comic entertainer, the might and magnificence of the gorillas stir us with awe. Second, beauty incarnate. Dian Fossey picked up where the movie left off. Hers was a 'Had Fay Wray done the right thing' story as she headed into the forest to discover all she could about the giant's gentle nature, then back out again to make it known the world over. Her landmark research has since inspired generations of scientists and conservationists, while the awareness she raised among the general public has helped steer the policies of decision-makers. Since Dian Fossey's day, leaps and bounds have been made in every field of research, from genetics, ecology and the neuro- and cognitive sciences to anthropology, animal behaviour and human behaviour. In addition, we are beginning in the Western

world to look closer at the research findings
coming from other parts of the world, for
example Asia, and discovering that other
approaches to research – indeed to life –

lead to areas of study and results that
we may hitherto have overlooked. Collating
and making sense of this vast and
ever-evolving diversity of material from every

field and every continent is a tremendous challenge, with equally tremendous implications. Linnaeus once wrote that he could "draw no principle from science by which it would be possible to distinguish Man from ape". It seems he was right and wrong. We are both like and unlike other apes. Where once we dismissed them because we could not teach them to speak, today we are willing to listen to what they have to tell us. In the light of what we are learning from gorillas and our other close relatives about their aptitude for language, tool use, bipedalism, empathy, cooperation, deceit, war and reconciliation, even trade, humour and art, we are obliged to continually redefine and reinvent ourselves as humans. But our world is changing and so is the gorilla's. The issues at stake today in the study and conservation of gorillas reach far beyond any interests of a fundamental nature we may have. From contemplation we must now act, and act fast, to secure our common future. Though the planet's forests are crucial to maintaining our air and freshwater supplies, turning carbon dioxide into oxygen and securing the patterns of rainfall that ensure the crops on which we humans depend, the rate of deforestation is accelerating. Fortunately, as people, governments, international institutions and corporations around the world begin to realise the global extent of the risks we run due to climate change, global solutions are being sought, and forests are

beginning to be viewed not just in their
transformation but as one of the key
components in maintaining the biosphere.
In the words of Ian Redmond, "Everyone
alive benefits but, so far, none of us have
paid for these services. Instead we have
mined the forest timber, eaten the forest
animals and converted the land to
agriculture. We have done so because
it has been more profitable than
conservation. So it is not surprising that
the concept of the world paying to keep
forests standing is being greeted with
excitement by ecologists and forest-

dwelling people alike." Africa's tropical
forests represent a significant share
of these life-supporting systems. In today's
global village of species, gorillas have
their own role to play as the keepers
of the forest. Gorillas are both a keystone
species on which the forest depends
to renew itself, and a flagship species
on which our hearts depend, for we too
are social apes and the plight of our close
cousins cannot leave us indifferent.
Even the silverback slows the pace
of his foraging group to allow the weaker
members to keep up.

A PUZZLING DISCOVERY

Many of our lasting impressions of gorillas have come down to us from reports written by early explorers and adventurers. Yet these observations are surprisingly recent, given the animals' size and human-like appearance. Prior to the late 16th century there is only a single account, dating from Antiquity.

In the 5th century BCE, Hanno the Navigator set sail from Carthage with a fleet of sixty ships to explore and colonize the west coast of Africa. Having run out of provisions they were about to turn back when they came to a bay with an island, probably in the vicinity of modern-day Gabon or Cameroon.

On the island was a lake and in that lake another island. This island, they claimed, was inhabited by a hirsute tribe, whom their interpreters called gorilla people.

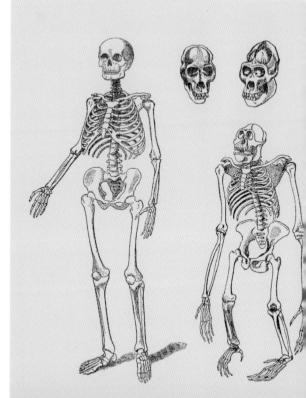

The first scientific evidence of the gorilla's existence came in the form of skeletons and skulls. There was no mistaking then their resemblance to those of humans and other apes, nor is there now.

The tradition of gorilla stamps around the world bears witness to the interest in gorillas both inside and outside the countries lucky enough to boast their presence.

The gorillas, most of whom were females, threw stones to defend themselves and the males escaped over the cliffs (behaviours which lead some to question whether these were the species we now know as gorillas). Hanno and his men nevertheless managed to capture three of the females, who fought tooth and nail until the only way to calm them, it seemed, was to kill them. An unchivalrous lot, the Carthaginians skinned these so-called 'women' and sailed home with their hairy pelts. The Western world would wait another 2,000 years for the next report. At the very end of the 16th century, the English privateer Andrew Battel was captured by the Portuguese and trailed through the forests

Few movie characters can lay claim to the durable success of King Kong, the last of a fictitious, prehistoric species called *Megaprimatus kong* discovered on the equally fictitious but ever so fascinating Skull Island.

of West Africa. It is clear from Battel's detailed account that he observed both chimpanzees and gorillas. This time, the indigenous people called the latter the 'pongo'. But for all its detail, could Battel's description be believed? This was the start of the golden age of exploration. New discoveries were being revealed daily, while established 'facts' were relegated to folklore. Without irrefutable proof, no one could safely say to which category the tales of giant apes belonged. It was not until 1847, almost 250 years later, that the first scientific description of the animal was given by the aptly named Dr. T. S. Savage, a missionary to the Congo and naturalist, who had already written about chimpanzees. While visiting Gabon, Savage came across a massive skull. Instantly, he recognized its significance. It was the skull of a new species. Thrilled at the

discovery, he commissioned local hunters to procure male and female skulls, pelvises and other bones. These he sent, along with a description of gorilla habits, to Jeffries Wyman, an anatomy professor at Harvard

The aptly named Dr. Savage gave the first scientific description

and the co-author of his chimpanzee article. The joint paper they presented to the Boston Journal of Natural History later that year was at last to take the creature out of the realm of legend. Savage and Wyman grouped their find together with the chimpanzee under the latter's generic name *Troglodytes*, adding Hanno the Navigator's term *gorilla* to identify the species. Why didn't they choose Battel's name *Pongo*? It had already been given to the orangutan. This ape is even more

Do Eastern and Western Gorillas differ as much as chimpanzees and bonobos? Genetic analyses are inexplicably contradictory. It may be that the two gorilla populations separated early on but that over the ages forest corridors have occasionally formed to allow some genetic mingling. The debate is still out.

distantly related to the gorilla than we are, but at one point in history all great apes were believed to be some form of orangutan, and hence were lumped under the most convenient name to hand: *Pongo*. While the orangutan's misnomer has stuck to this day, *Troglodytes* was quickly dropped as a genus for both (it had already been used for the tiny wren!) and gorillas were renamed quite simply *Gorilla gorilla*. Once the gorilla's existence had finally been confirmed, everybody wanted one. In Richard Burton's 1876 book *Two Trips to Gorilla Land and the Cataracts of the Congo*, he quotes a local hunter who boasted that, since demand had risen, he had supplied a single European trader with an average of one gorilla a month, including a live infant. Circuses, zoos and museums, not to mention trophy hunters, wanted to display them, dead or alive depending on their profession. Naturalists, on the other

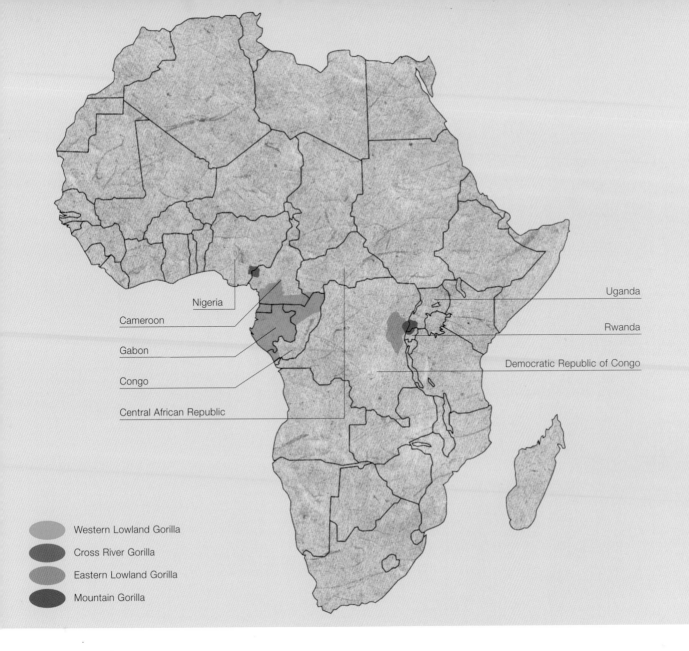

Western Lowland Gorilla

Cross River Gorilla

Eastern Lowland Gorilla

Mountain Gorilla

Nigeria

Cameroon

Gabon

Congo

Central African Republic

Uganda

Rwanda

Democratic Republic of Congo

hand, seemed only to want to name them. New gorilla species and subspecies began popping up in museums and scientific journals at an alarming rate. The German Paul Matschie was especially prolific. Quick on the draw when his compatriot Captain Robert von Beringe shot the first Mountain Gorillas, he named six gorilla species in all, prompted the naming of a seventh, and had yet another named after himself. By the early 20th century, the number of gorilla species

had become unmanageable. Attempts to reign in their number began around the time that the film *King Kong* was released. Yet even now, the line is a hard one to draw.

We base our definitions of species partly on measurable or observable characteristics, such as morphology and more recently behaviour, and partly on genetic factors. As our knowledge increases, this information is constantly revised. The truth is, our understanding evolves much like species

themselves. Since 2001, there has never-theless been a general consensus that gorillas belong to one of two different species, each divided in turn into two subspecies:

– Western Gorillas:

Western Lowland Gorilla – *Gorilla gorilla gorilla* (Savage & Wyman, 1847) and Cross River Gorilla – *Gorilla gorilla diehli* (Matschie, 1903);

– Eastern Gorillas:

Mountain Gorilla – *Gorilla beringei beringei* (Matschie, 1903) and Eastern Lowland Gorilla – *Gorilla beringei graueri* (Matschie, 1914).

So far, Matschie's zeal has paid off.

Of the four gorillas, three still bear the names he gave them. Gorillas were once much more numerous than they are today. During the last Ice Age, a major portion of the rainforest disappeared, dividing the populations in the west and the east by more than 1,000 km. The four types of gorilla are now distributed

of the Cross River on either side of the Nigeria-Cameroon border. Fortunately, the few surviving Cross River Gorillas are fairly isolated from their human neighbours and improved conservation is reducing the risk from hunting. Of the two Eastern species, the most populous is the Eastern Lowland Gorilla with a 1996 estimate of 17,000 living in eastern DRC. A decade of war and turmoil, coupled with unregulated mining of coltan and tin to feed international demand

We have the Mountain Gorillas to thank for the creation of Africa's first National Park

along a patchy belt that stretches from equatorial west to east central Africa, separated by the northward curve of the Congo River and its tributaries. Those first encountered by Dr. Savage – and no doubt Hanno and Battel – were Western Lowland Gorillas, which occur in Angola, Cameroon, Central African Republic, Congo, Equatorial Guinea, Gabon, Nigeria, and the far west of the Democratic Republic of Congo (DRC). Despite being the most numerous, less remote populations are plummeting due to the growing bush meat trade and the spread of disease, especially ebola. In contrast, by the time the Cross River Gorilla was recently acknowledged as a subspecies, it was already the rarest of the four, with a population of just 250 to 300 individuals. This gorilla is confined to a pocket of rugged highland forest on the upper drainage

from the electronics industry, is feared to have reduced this number by half (it is still too dangerous for surveys). Despite its name, it lives not only at low altitudes but can also be found in mountain forests up to almost 3,000 m. Last but not least, the Mountain Gorilla lives nearby where the borders of DRC, Uganda and Rwanda meet. The population of only some 720 is confined to two small areas in these countries. We have the Mountain Gorillas to thank for the creation of Africa's first National Park, now the Virunga National Park (DRC) as well as the Volcanoes National Park (Rwanda), and the Mgahinga Gorilla National Park (Uganda), all three of which are in the Virgunga range and a bit further away, the Bwindi Impenetrable Forest (also Uganda). Would, for the gorillas' sake, that all their forests were impenetrable.

In 1996, Western Lowland Gorillas were estimated at 95,000. Fortunately in 2008 new surveys of previously unexplored areas revised the figure upwards to 200,000. They are nevertheless critically endangered.

STINGUISHING FEATURES

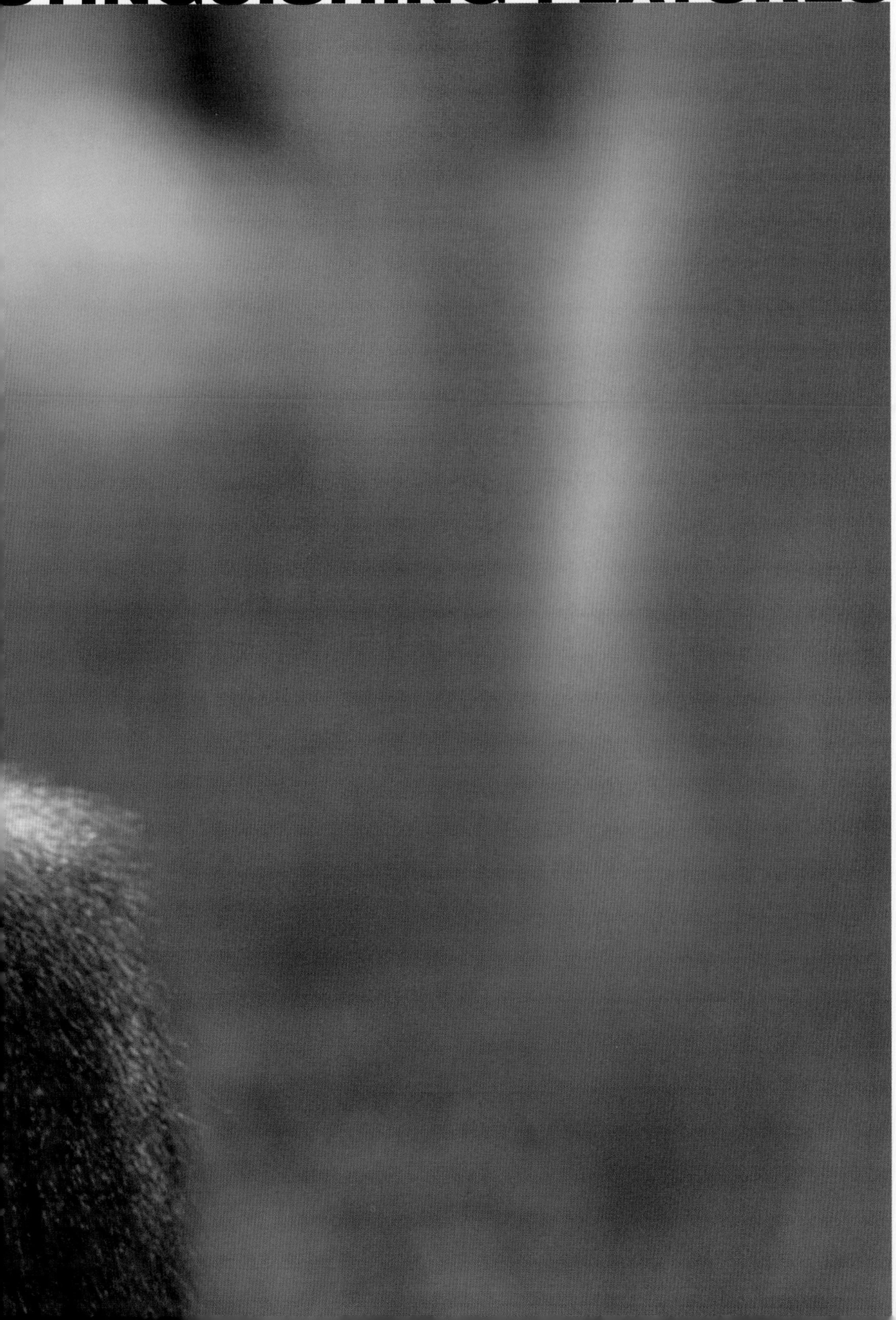

Left: Mountain Gorilla
with its signature dense
black coat. Middle:
Western Gorilla with
overhanging nose tip
and pronounced brow.
Right: Eastern Lowland
Gorilla, the largest of all.

to their fibrous diet. All gorillas have bare faces, palms and soles and bluish- or brownish-black skin, though infants are often born with pink-grey skin that darkens quickly. Young gorillas have hairy chests but at puberty, females lose the hair on their breasts and males lose the hair on the whole front of their chest. There are subtle – and some not so subtle – differences between the gorilla races. The most easily recognizable is undoubtedly

The most easily recognizable is the Mountain Gorilla

Gorillas are the largest of all living primates. Because they sometimes stand upright like humans and have no tail, they are measured in terms of height rather than head and body or tail length like most mammals. Adult male gorillas range from 140 to 185 cm tall and weigh an average of 160 kg. Females are small by comparison at a maximum height of 150 cm, and weigh about 70 to 115 kg. Both sexes are easy to distinguish from chimpanzees by their more robust build, broad chest, small ears and prominent pot-belly.

Whereas chimpanzees have conspicuous genitals, those of gorillas are so hard to spot that it can be difficult to tell young males from young females. Gorillas' legs are short but they have long, powerful arms, which they sometimes use to pull over small trees. Their teeth are as robust as the rest of their build, an adaptation

the Mountain Gorilla, with its long glossy coat which helps to keep it warm and dry in the chilly montane forest it inhabits. This thick black hair, which closely frames its broad face and massive jaws, makes it appear the largest of the gorillas. In reality, its closest relative, the Eastern Lowland Gorilla, holds all the records, with reports of large male silverbacks in the wild weighing in at 225 kg, with an arm span of over 2.5 m. Like the Mountain Gorilla, its coat is predominantly black though not quite as long and thick. The slighter build of the Western races enables them to spend more time in the trees than their cousins. Their body hair is less dense and of a lighter brown. Some individuals are even redheads. But the best way to identify a Western Gorilla is to take a close look at its nose; only they have an overhanging tip. Gorillas are among the most sexually dimorphic

of any primate. This means that, at a glance, it is easy to tell adult males from females. Infant males lag behind females in terms of early growth spurts, and as they grow they may be difficult to tell apart, but fully grown males weigh a whopping twice as much as their sisters and mates. In Mountain Gorillas, the contrast in size between males and females is even greater. But size is not the only way to tell the sexes apart. As they mature, males develop a prominent, conical head, a prominent

While differences between silverbacks and females are obvious, and those between individuals are marked, mothers and their offspring often bear a striking family resemblance.

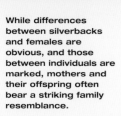

brow, powerful jaws and formidable canines. They also develop a distinctive 'saddle' of silvery grey hair that extends from the back to the rump and thighs, hence the name 'silverbacks'. Presumably, the more distinct these traits are in a male, the more attractive he is to mates. 'Manliness' is not the only identifying characteristic, even in silverbacks. Each gorilla has its own distinct facial features, habits and personality. Researchers generally use drawings or photographs to identify individual gorillas by the 'nose-print' – the pattern formed by folds of skin above the nose, at least until they become familiar with the more subtle clues. Gorillas, on the other hand, make out individual traits instantly and, in the case of Western Gorillas, they recognize family, friends and foe even after long periods of separation. In addition, gorillas appear to have their own taste when it comes to attractive features in a fellow gorilla. Koko, the captive gorilla famous for learning sign language,

Each gorilla has its own distinct facial features

was shown a series of videos with different silverbacks from zoos as possible mates. When Ndume appeared on the screen, Koko leaned over to kiss him!

Ancient history can be traced in the gorilla's morphology. Primates were one of the earliest orders of mammal, preceded only by carnivores and the shrew-like insectivores

from which they diverged. The oldest primate fossil we have is a molar from *Purgatorius ceratops*, discovered in Purgatory, Montana and named in honour of its illustrious dinosaur contemporary, the triceratops. Despite the 66 million years that have since passed, the overall pattern of flexible behaviour and generalized

morphology of primates is evident in such divergent primates as mouse-lemurs and gorillas. So little have we changed in fact that it can be hard to pinpoint just what differentiates modern primates from other mammals: the structure of the inner ear, perforations at the base of the cranium, the shape of their molars and rounded

Of all the apes, gorillas' hands and feet most resemble our own. Hence our surprise at the manipulative skill they demonstrate when suddenly grasping food or anything else with their feet. Far left: The grey saddle for which silverbacks are named.

cusps, the way they are able to sit, and some even stand. What really makes primates special is, paradoxically, their lack of specialisation. Whereas creatures that are too highly specialised cannot keep pace with changing environments, the primate order owes its success to its behavioural and physical adaptability. Gorillas are no exception. Though they are limited in range to tropical forests, they can be found napping in the trees of muggy swamps or leading an almost purely terrestrial life in chilly montane forests. They prefer fruit but when there is none they feed on tough vegetation. Their opposable thumbs, which developed to serve primates in the trees (as well as, independently, the big toes of pandas, koalas and opossums), have been literally instrumental in adapting their lifestyles and even diets. Gorilla hands look very much like our own, including

the fingernails, but with stubby fingers and a shorter thumb. As for their feet, gorillas can still curl their toes and use their big toe to grasp objects with remarkable dexterity. In this they have a certain advantage over us, at least as long as they are living the rainforest life and not sporting trainers and running marathons!

Just how would a gorilla run a marathon? On all fours, no doubt. They are the most terrestrial of the apes, and their gait is primarily quadrupedal. Yet anatomically, they are not especially well equipped for life on the ground. Though they walk with the soles of their feet planted firmly on the ground, the weight of their forequarters rests on the back of the middle phalanges of their curled fingers. Other terrestrial monkeys, like baboons and macaques, walk on the flats of their fingers with open palms. The gorilla's 'knucklewalking' is a form of compromise, shared by chimpanzees, that allows them to use their hands for terrestrial locomotion while keeping their long fingers, which are needed for climbing and preparing food. In knucklewalking, the wrist locks into place helping to support the animal's weight. Because their arms are longer than their legs, gorillas may appear semi-upright. There is some recent fossil evidence that our human ancestors may also once have walked on their knuckles, before evolving toward our current bipedal stance.

Gorillas do occasionally stand on two feet. This is particularly true during chest-beating displays, when male gorillas have been observed to run bipedally up to 6 m. But gorilla body structure, especially in the heavy adults, does not allow them

to stand for any length of time. As humans we are built for full-time bipedalism. The shape of our pelvis in particular enables us to balance ourselves upright above straight legs. Gorillas can straighten their legs, but their centre of gravity is far forward, causing them to tip at the hip joints. Gorillas can counteract this using their

The gorilla's 'knucklewalking' is a form of compromise

hamstring muscles, but to do so they have to bend their knees. To sustain an upright position, a whole series of mechanisms comes into play, which in the final count are simply not worth the extra effort to the gorilla.

What comes naturally to gorillas has inspired scientists in Japan to achieve a feat of robotics. The 'gorilla robot' is capable of switching from quadrupedalism to bipedalism to brachiation, and may eventually have far-reaching applications because of its ability to adapt its locomotion to its environment, though it cannot mimic the grace of its model.

We tend to be fascinated with any ape's ability to walk upright because we generally consider it to be a human trademark. Ape bipedalism sheds light on our own ancient ancestry and theories abound as to just how it first developed. It is generally accepted that our common ancestors descended from the trees and went through a quadrupedal phase on all fours before ever standing upright. Recent research on orangutans has led to another hypothesis, in which the ancestors of today's apes actually began to stand while still in the trees. Orangutans diverged from the ape family tree very early on. They have remained the most arboreal of the apes. Even their form of knucklewalking is less suited to a terrestrial lifestyle, since they bear their weight on the outer fists rather than the phalanges. They almost never walk upright on the ground unless prompted. However we now know they often walk carefully on two feet along fragile branches, using their hands to grasp branches overhead and maintain their balance, as do gibbons. If bipedalism was indeed an early trait in hominids, it just may be that gorillas, as the most terrestrial apes at the opposite end of the spectrum from orangutans, are losing, rather than developing, bipedal habits.

One of the primates' chief adaptations to life in the trees was the vertical position they required to cling to tree trunks. Strange as it sounds, one of the prerequisites to bipedalism may very well be brachiation, that is, the capacity to travel hand over hand, suspended from branches. We can see for ourselves how arm swinging in both forms of locomotion shows similar left, right, left, right sequences. Only the lesser apes (gibbons and siamangs) are true brachiators. Nevertheless, gorillas and the other great apes, not to mention humans, have retained the anatomical features such as long arms, flexible

A prerequisite to bipedalism may be brachiation

shoulders, wide chests, and prehensile hands that theoretically should enable us all to swing through the trees like Tarzan. But with the exception of orangutans, we other hominids have our reasons for seldom doing so. For gorillas, it is a question of sheer size. Because they are lighter, young gorillas and the occasional adult female will hang from an arm while foraging or clowning about. In general, Western Gorillas, young or old, male or female are good vertical climbers, though once again, adult females, because of their lighter weight, tend to spend more time in the trees. Though fully grown silverbacks virtually never swing from a branch, they do climb trees, especially when fruit is in season. When silverbacks decide to use their age-old morphological features to haul their heavy-weight bodies up a tree, they do so very, very cautiously but sometimes with amazing grace and balance for an animal so large.

YOU ARE WHAT YOU EAT

If Aesop were to rewrite *The Grasshopper and the Ant* using primates, he might call his fable *The Ape and the Monkey*. Indeed it seems that the apes' attachment to the good life, warm temperatures, swinging in trees and a constant supply of ripe fruit may have led to the decline in their diversity as this type of habitat became increasingly hard to come by. Meanwhile, the old world monkeys varied their diets and habits and species, expanding into new terrain unsuitable for the fussier apes. It is likely that our own human ancestors followed the monkeys in this respect, taking definitive leave of the ancestral apes that evolved into orangutans, chimpanzees and, of course, gorillas, who would gradually become restricted to equatorial forest. Great apes are fundamentally tree-climbing, fruit-eating

As the most terrestrial of apes, gorillas forage largely on the ground, especially when fruit is not available.
The forest they inhabit is dense, but not so much that it blocks out the light that sustains the rich understory of plant life on which the gorillas depend.

While most gorillas live in warm moist forest, the Mountain Gorillas have adapted to the high altitudes where night-time temperatures can fall below freezing and dense cloud cover blankets the moss, lichens, ferns, orchids and other epiphytes that grow on trees.

animals, as were our ancestors for the most part. During the Miocene – the heyday of great ape diversity – apes ranged across not only Africa but also Eurasia.

Our common ancestor most likely arose and diverged from animals that had already left Africa (though some recent fossil evidence points to the contrary) and were subsequently forced southward again to escape a cooling climate and the changing food supply that comes with changing seasons: orangutan ancestors were pushed into south-east Asia while human/chimpanzee and gorilla ancestors headed back to Africa. Gorillas nevertheless retained the trademark adaptability of primates as a whole. For instance, though

During the Miocene apes ranged across Africa and Eurasia

there are few encounters between gorillas and chimpanzees, even in restricted areas, there is quite a bit of overlap in habitat. It seems likely that when it came to foraging for fruit in shrinking warm, moist forest, the lithe, smaller chimpanzee ancestor had a decisive advantage over the more cumbersome gorilla ancestor. Gorillas therefore adapted their feeding strategies to take advantage of the forest's herbaceous and woody understory, making it possible for them to extend into unexpected terrain such as the Virunga Volcano range, where it is too cold for most tropical fruits.

Chimpanzees are not the gorilla's only neighbours. The Congo basin alone is home to 1,000 known bird species and 400 mammal species. The African Jacana is one species of bird that actually prefers foraging close to gorillas. Other primates abound in the ranges of the Lowland Gorillas, including the striking black and white colobus once sought after for its long silky coat, and the surprising mandrill with its vivid blue and red face. The golden monkey, recently recognized as a distinct

In the western lowlands, marshy clearings known as bais provide edible grasses and starchy sedges for the forest's large but secretive herbivores including the gorillas, not to mention rare opportunities for observing them out in the open. By defecating seeds and disturbing the wet they actually maintain it for future use.

species, has even made it as high as the Mountain Gorilla. Gorillas share the forest with a number of other large forest herbivores, often coming into contact with forest buffalo, the elusive bongos, and forest elephants. This subspecies of African elephant (some now consider it a separate species) is substantially smaller than the better known bush elephant, with comparatively straight, downward-pointing tusks and, usually, an extra toenail on each of its four feet. In some areas, the forest elephant can, like the chimpanzee, prove competition for desirable fruit stores. On the other hand, it knocks down trees and uses traditional pathways through the forest, creating just the kind of clearing that fosters growth of low, edible new-growth vegetation that gorillas appreciate.

The two populations that make up today's 720 estimated Mountain Gorillas are roughly

Edible plants are not as diverse in Mountain Gorilla country

divided between the forested slopes and high valleys of dormant Virunga Volcanoes and, some 25 miles north, the much lower Bwindi Impenetrable Forest. The latter has teetered unchanged on the edge of the Albertine Rift Valley since before the last Ice Age. Both areas are characterized by Afromontane forest; in the Virungas, the gorillas favour the belt of towering *Hagenia* trees and flowering *Hypericum* that occurs above the line of bamboo and below Afroalpine meadows, which have little to offer in the way of gorilla food. Edible plants are not as diverse in Mountain Gorilla country as they are in Western Lowland Gorilla areas – about 60 and 200 plant species respectively – but they are plentiful. Mountain Gorillas need only reach out to grab a handful of the scraggly but abundant vine called *Galium*, or carefully prepare thistles or wild celery that make up the bulk of their diet by far. Fruits, mainly two varieties of blackberry, make up only two per cent of their diet. But this diet is lacking in certain vitamins and minerals.

To supplement it, they also eat roots, bark and occasionally ants, and sometimes even soil or their own dung. At the opposite end of the spectrum, the diverse habitats occupied by the Western Lowland Gorillas, from flooded forest and swampland to hillside forest and riversides, provide them with the most varied diet of all. Indeed, over 200 species and varieties of plants and 100 species and varieties of fruit have been identified. Of these species, even more different plant parts are consumed. Fruits rank top in terms of variety, vegetation in terms of bulk. To complicate matters further, their diet varies according to season, to group tradition and to individual taste. Generally speaking, Western Gorilla plant foods belong to one of three categories: staple foods which they tend to eat year round (piths, leaves, roots and shoots from nutritious sources); a large variety of ripe fruits they consume with relish when in season; and what are called 'fallback' foods – less nutritious foods they'll eat at a pinch. Western Gorillas also eat insects, mainly ants and termites, and other invertebrates on occasion. They do not, as far as we know, use tools to get at them like chimpanzees do. Nor, despite their eclectic diet, do they eat eggs or meat like chimpanzees, much to the dismay of the first gorilla keepers at the New York Zoological Society who, in 1912, saw their new ward refuse a meat dish served hot from New York City's Rockingstone Restaurant! Among the plants on which

It was long thought that all gorillas were strict consumers of vegetation, but Western Lowland Gorillas also consume large amounts of fruit. Mountain Gorillas, it turns out, eat their greens because that's all they've got.

wild Western Gorillas largely subsist is a genus of wild ginger called *Aframomum*. In the swampy lowlands of West Africa's Grain Coast the preferred species is the leafy, palm-like *Aframomum melegueta*. Standing almost as tall as a gorilla, with trumpet-shaped flowers, its seeds are valued as a precious spice. Medieval spice traders claimed they grew only in Eden, hence the plant's common name 'grains of paradise'. Offering the peppery spice with floral overtones to guests is part of West African hospitality. Native healers have long used it to treat anything from coughs to measles. Grains of paradise, it turns out, form an anti-bacterial, antiviral, antifungal and anti-inflammatory wonder drug. Doctors outside Africa are beginning to catch on. So are zoo veterinarians. While *Aframomum* constitutes a large share of a wild gorilla's diet, captive gorillas don't get any. What they do get is a heart condition, fibrosing cardiomyopathy. Fortunately for gorillas and humans alike,

Western Lowland Gorillas do not hesitate to climb high into trees for fruit, or wade right into swamp water for sedges, while Mountain Gorillas are usually content to reach out and grab a handful of nettles or celery, unless of course they come across a rare fruiting tree, when they too climb.

The music of the Aka as a whole falls under UNESCO's Intangible Heritage programme. The songs of the Ba'Aka are often one-lined polyphonic odes to their environment: "The forest is good".

zoos are looking at bringing the African plants back into the diets of gorillas, and pharmaceutical companies are investigating their potential as a powerful anti-inflammatory and cardio-medicine. For the moment, wild gorillas hold nature's patent: grains of paradise must pass through the gorilla's digestive system before they can germinate. While Mountain Gorillas are able to consume very little fruit, it accounts

in good part for the extraordinary diversity of the Western Lowland Gorilla diet. One favourite is the fruit of the Detarium, a woody species sometimes used in place of mahogany. This oily fruit, like others, tends to drip. Some populations of gorillas have found they can avoid a sticky mess by wiping their face, hands and fur free of it, and of other fruit spills, by using leaves. They'll reach for any leaf handy

The Ba'Aka people look for leafy napkins tossed aside

– the bigger the better – but they prefer the large leaves of local arrowroot. When trailing gorillas, the Ba'Aka people look for leafy napkins tossed aside as proof they are on the right track. The Ba'Aka, who share the forest with gorillas on such intimate terms, are one of the many tribes that make up the group for which there is as yet no better term than pygmies, and whose small stature is due to deficient assimilation of growth hormones.

Their nomadic communities include anywhere from 30 to 100 members, and families construct thatched, dome-shaped habitations. They are surprisingly gentle and egalitarian, with men and women sharing in child care and whole communities of men, women and children banding together to 'net hunt', driving a quarry of game like duikers, small forest antelope, into rings of nets. Women do most of the gathering, filling their baskets with plants and beetles, yams and turtles, nuts, fungi, caterpillars and whatever other tasty morsels they happen across. Men collect honey and hunt larger prey like monkeys using poisoned darts and bows and arrows. They hunt even larger prey, including forest elephants and gorillas, with spears. No one knows the forest better. That is why when the Ba'Aka dwell on the edge of villages or forest concessions, other communities hire them – for next to nothing – to supply bushmeat for their markets. On a more positive note, it also explains why since scientists and conservationists began calling on them to assist in tracking Western Lowland Gorillas, research and

Waterways provide the Ba'Aka with fish, the gorillas with extensive belts of lush undergrowth, and offer both a refreshing way to travel through the sweltering heat of the forest.

habituation efforts have made significant headway. Fortunately for the Mountain Gorillas, the communities that have lived longest close to their sanctuaries do not eat ape meat. While there were fears that with war refugees and militia from other areas crowding into the region there would be poaching, this has been less of a concern than expected, though Eastern Lowland Gorillas have suffered tremendous losses. Paradoxically, Mountain Gorilla populations have actually increased during the last two

The volcanic soil that flanks the Virungas is among the richest in Africa

decades of human strife in the area. The volcanic soil that flanks the Virungas is among the richest in Africa. Crops grow in plenty. As might be expected, the human population is correspondingly dense and is bound to become more so. Unlike much of Africa, where the tsetse fly plagues humans with sleeping sickness and cattle with nagana and pigs with sura, livestock thrives at the higher, fly-free altitudes. This good land is much sought after, and although people occasionally set a snare to catch small game (gorillas lose hands to snares) the majority are by tradition farmers, not hunters. Farm they do, right up to the edge of the forest, so close in fact that the Mountain Gorillas sometimes picnic on their crops. This is the only glimpse that most of the animals' human neighbours and cousins are ever likely to get.

There is no buffer zone around Volcanoes National Park. Programmes to improve community infrastructure and education keep children in school and out of the park where they and their parents go to collect firewood and other commodities.

THE GOOD LIFE

Western Gorillas were the first to be discovered by science, described head to toe, and held in captivity. Yet until recently, most of what we know about gorilla ecology and behaviour in the wild has been based on studies of the Mountain Gorilla. These began in 1959 with the trail-blazing Dr. George Schaller, followed in 1967 by the famed Dian Fossey. Little could she have known that her story would one day become the stuff of a Hollywood blockbuster named after her book, *Gorillas in the Mist*. Even so, it did not take long for Dian Fossey and the first of the Mountain Gorillas she would study for the next 19 years to become household names; National Geographic Society was funding the work and after a couple of years sent photographer and filmmaker Bob Campbell to document her progress.

If you want to observe most animals in the wild, you try to avoid being observed yourself, the reason being that if the animal sees you, its behaviour will change.

To know gorillas you must first let them know you

Above right: Infant gorillas today in a zoo-sponsored re-introduction programme.
Right: In 1969, Dian Fossey nursed Coco and Pucker, whose mothers were killed to capture them for a zoo. She fought hard to keep them in the Virungas but the zoo won.

Fossey, determined to observe uninhibited gorilla behaviour, requested that Campbell keep his distance, despite visibility that was next to none. "To habituate the mountain gorillas was overstepping the mark as far as the behaviourists were concerned, even though they too were missing out on an awful lot because of the heavy foliage,"

says Campbell. But after 15 months of non-intrusive work, he realized he would have to persuade Fossey to let him move his cameras in closer. At last she relented. "I used a very careful technique which was getting down on my hands and knees and behaving like a gorilla," recalls Campbell, "soon we discovered that gorillas are very tolerant". The unexpected bonus was that once the gorillas accepted the close approaches, they got on with their lives and the quality of observations improved dramatically. If you want to get to know gorillas, it turns out, you must first let them get to know you. Habituation of the Mountain Gorillas has also led to the tourism

When habituating
Western Lowland
Gorillas, contacting
them in trees or thick
forest gives them
a sense of security and
achieves the best
results.

so crucial to ensure governmental and local endorsement of conservation programmes. Inspired by the success with Mountain Gorillas, there have been steady attempts since the 1990s to habituate Western Lowland Gorilla groups. But during this same time, hunting for the bushmeat trade has skyrocketed. Whereas a silverback will take on a leaping leopard to defend his females, gorillas with past poacher experience will flee for miles. Habituation has therefore proven excruciatingly slow, even with help from the Ba'Aka. Nevertheless, the studies it has helped to achieve are beginning to bear fruit – surprising fruit at that – and we are learning more about the similarities and differences between these close cousins. In the warm lowland forest where sunlight seldom penetrates, gorillas have little

"Over three decades ago, habituating three wild mountain gorilla families to accept a close human presence was both intensely exciting and rewarding; exciting because of not knowing what to expect from powerful and potentially dangerous creatures reluctant to be approached, and rewarding when a high degree of mutual trust developed so quickly. The peak of the habituating process comes when your subjects choose of their own accord to interact with you. Rough and tumble bouts of play instigated by a wild gorilla all those years ago have left indelible memories. It was with great reluctance that I had to take steps to discourage them. Most of the Virunga gorillas are now so thoroughly habituated to the human presence they tolerate being stared at by the eyes and lenses of large groups of people. Most primates express emotions and intentions with their eyes; they must experience some strange feelings about the direct and rude stares of the humans."
Bob Campbell, photographer, documentary film maker and author of The Taming of the Gorillas.

cause to sleep in. But at daybreak on
a cold misty morning in the Virungas, they
may well huddle until the chill dissipates,
just as on those mornings when the mist
burns off early, they stay in bed to soak up
the sun. They'll all be up within the hour.
Breakfast awaits. Gorillas spend 30 to 45
per cent of their day feeding and about
30 per cent travelling. The rest is devoted
to leisure, with naps a cherished pastime.
Across species and within groups, they
all follow roughly the same schedule.
Three to four hours of feeding and foraging,

then play for the young and socialising
and siesta for all, followed by more
foraging, after which it is time to build
a nest and settle down at day's last light.
While foraging, gorillas are constantly
on the go, stopping when favourite foods
are found and making the rounds to check
on the state of feeding haunts from years
past. In the botanically diverse forest they
inhabit, Western Lowland Gorillas easily
travel several kilometres in the course
of a day – much more than Mountain
Gorillas. When they visit swamps and bai

After foraging
in the morning hours,
gorillas take time out
to socialise.

clearings, they may extend their day range by 50 per cent. The fact that the underbrush beneath the thick canopy of their forests is less dense than in the Virungas or Bwindi means that food sources are patchy, but it also means it is easier to move unhampered in search of them. Part of what they are looking for is fruiting trees. When they find them they will climb to any height to get to them, at times demonstrating dazzling acrobatics, even hanging upside down high in the canopy. Who hangs where is a question of size, social rank and tree structure. Silverbacks rarely venture as high as females and juveniles, or onto smaller branches.

Nor do they often deign to use suspensory behaviour. As on the ground, they pull rank, posting themselves in choice positions in the cores of trees and on the large, sturdy branches. Females on the other hand, and to a lesser extent lower-ranking males, do use risky postures and smaller and sometimes multiple branches, foraging in the periphery of trees. Despite this hierarchy, competition is not a common trait of gorillas and when males and females forage together they use large trees where everyone can gain access. Even when feeding on the ground adults prefer to put distance between themselves, sometimes dividing into subgroups for periods of time. During fruit-poor seasons, when silverbacks

Competition is not a common trait of gorillas

don't bother to climb much at all, females use the more secure spots. When males are on their own, they actually prefer trees with small crowns where they need not 'go out on a limb' to reach the abundant fruit on outer branches. Sliding down an arm-thick vine to reach the ground, the group may move on to a swamp to root out swamp plants, rinsing them off and slurping them down. Mountain Gorillas sit regally pulling out handfuls of plants all around them, but their four most common foods actually require precision processing to expose the palatable parts. Indeed, getting past

Gorillas are not territorial. This silverback bears wounds from a battle he would have fought to defend his females and infants, never over food.

An individual's technique continues to improve into adulthood

the stings, hooks and spines that 'defend' these foods requires combining several actions into a complex sequence. Deftly stripping a stem of stinging nettle leaves, removing the petioles, folding them into a little parcel with the sting-less underside of a leaf facing outward without getting stung requires great dexterity and skill that only seems simple because experienced gorillas do it with such ease. It actually involves a steep learning curve that gorillas begin to master by the time they are weaned, at about 3½ years. An individual's technique continues to improve into adulthood, when he or she develops hand preferences for each step of the process

In swampy areas, Western Lowland Gorillas spend time foraging for sedges and other aquatic plants.

Gorilla facial expressions closely resemble those of chimpanzees and our own. However, other apes for the most part hide their teeth when they smile or laugh. Exposed gums as in this yawn (above middle) may express uneasiness.

and learns to adapt it to circumstances. While gorillas have been pooh-poohed for not using aimed blows with rocks or other objects to get into food, like chimpanzees, the sequences involved in food processing may reflect even higher cognitive capability, at least when it comes to manual skills. Naps and bedtime involve another interesting behaviour. Nine out of ten Mountain Gorillas build nests to sleep in at night and most of them do so in the afternoon. These are primarily for individuals but two gorillas will occasionally bunk together. Infants share their mother's nest until they are three years old or until the arrival of a sibling pushes them out, though they begin playing at nest building at around eight months. Nests are clustered at sites chosen on the basis of available materials and are rarely re-used. Western Gorillas in swampy areas often build nests using *Aframomum*, the plant with all-encompassing medicinal properties. To build a proper nest, a gorilla pulls up, breaks off or bends over any suitable vines, branches or other plant materials,

and tucks them underneath and around itself to form a roughly circular padding. On the ground, the effort goes into forming a rim. When nests are built in trees, usually in the forks or along broad horizontal branches, the builders stress stronger bottom support. Studies on Western Lowland Gorillas show that they do not build nests all the time, and prefer to sleep on the bare ground when the weather is hot. When they do build nests, females, blackbacks and juveniles build more in the trees than do silverbacks. They build even

more in trees if they have lost their protector silverback, but when a new one immigrates, the females especially return quickly to nest near him on the ground. Nests are of interest to conservationists, who use them to count Mountain Gorillas. But other gorillas share the forests with chimpanzees, whose nests are so similar they cannot be told apart 75 per cent of the time. Whether foraging, travelling or lounging, in a tree or on the ground, gorillas communicate using a combination of vocalisations, non-vocal sounds, and visual signals and expressions. Originally described in relation to Mountain Gorillas

Gorillas spend almost a third of their time resting thoughtfully, but shall we ever know what they are thinking?

by Schaller and Fossey, this holds true for other gorillas. Adult males are by far the most vocal. Indeed they account for about 90 per cent of all gorilla vocalisations. Of the loud calls specific to males, hoot

Adult males are by far the most vocal

Day after day of watching its mother build daytime and nightime nests will one day help this infant build its own, though it will need time to perfect its technique.

series – repetitions of low but distinct hoo-hoo-hoos coupled with the silverback's loud chest-beat – carry far and alert outside groups to another's presence. Hoot series are made with the mouth parted, the lips pursed. They build up in volume and lengthen as they are repeated, then slur together as a rapid tattoo is pounded on the chest. Hooting in this way almost always serves as a prelude to chest-beating, or to other displays such as breaking branches, slapping the ground (or the water in the case of swamp gorillas) or a more daunting combination sequence whereby a male hoots, then rising onto two feet, snatches handfuls of vegetation and flings them wildly about, slaps his chest with one cupped hand after the other and kicks a leg into the air. The climax can occur within five seconds, but the display might roll on for another 30 seconds or so, as he sidesteps a few feet, whacking the undergrowth (and sometimes walloping any member of the group unfortunate enough to be in the way), tearing off branches and thumping on the ground with an open palm as he goes.

While all gorillas beat their chests, females and infants included, only adult males produce the hollow 'pok-pok-pok', using cupped hands against the bare skin of the chest beneath the pectoral muscle. The sound is amplified by the large air sacs on their throat.

When silverbacks or mature blackbacks perceive a severe threat, usually in response to human disturbance, they let out a blood-curdling roar. Paul du Chaillu's description from this 1861 account is still accurate: "The roar of the gorilla is the most singular and awful noise heard in these African woods. It begins with a sharp bark, like an angry dog, then glides into a deep bass

When a silverback roars, it's time for the group to rally

roll, which literally and closely resembles the roll of distant thunder along the sky, for which I have sometimes been tempted to take it where I did not see the animal. So deep is it that it seems to proceed less from the mouth and throat than from the deep chest and vast paunch."

When a silverback roars, it's time for the group to rally behind for protection. Not all vocalizations and displays are so spectacular. Gorillas may express alarm through hoot barks, which generally urge the group to move off. Question barks are a way of asking "who goes there?" at the sound of unfamiliar rustling in the trees. Hiccup barks express more curiosity than alarm, while growls or pig grunts express mild aggression among group members. When infant gorillas cry they could be mistaken for humans, though they usually only do so when left alone.

Infants and males alike will whine if injured or abandoned. On the other hand chuckles, rasping exhalations at play that are akin to laughter, are the second most common vocalisation. The most frequent, and the most complex, is the belch. Belch vocalisations such as soft grunting sometimes extend into 'singing' - soft humming, purring, and moaning sounds which express contentment, for instance after a long sunny day in the otherwise misty, chilly Virunga Mountains, or when sitting amongst a wealth of favourite foods. A group might croon in chorus before resuming foraging where they left off before a nap. Body language is just as important. The most straightforward is the strutting walk in which the gorilla literally struts its stuff. This stance and gait are used to affirm dominance. The gorilla assumes a stiff posture with arms bowed to best show off their powerful length, bristles its coat and stands sideways to look all the bigger. Sometimes two rivals will face off – or rather side off – and the excitement becomes tangible as infants watch, ready

Stealing a glance
can tell a gorilla a lot

to make a game of imitating them.
To make an impression, the strutting walk
has to be seen, and so it is reserved
for clearings or anywhere else the gorilla
is sure to have a good audience.
Nevertheless it is always a show of dignity,
the gorilla merely glancing out of the corner
of an eye to verify its impact.
Gorillas are highly sensitive to what they
read in the eyes of their fellow gorillas,

and of humans. Staring is rude, aggressive
behaviour in gorilla society, but stealing
a glance can tell a gorilla a lot.
They are also very sensitive to the reactions
of others, as well as highly skilled at reading
their intentions. In a two-part experiment
with captive gorillas, a human first simply
looked at the ceiling or straight ahead and
the gorilla's gaze followed. If they could not
figure out what the human was looking at
(usually because the experimenter wasn't
looking at anything special), the gorillas
looked back as if to double-check whether

they had correctly interpreted the human's gaze. In the second part of the experiment, the human looked at something behind an obstacle. The gorillas positioned themselves so they too had a view, though from a different angle, of what the human was looking at. Simple as this may seem, it means that gorillas are able to take the visual cue of another, thus revealing complex, flexible thought processes. They also know that others can read them too, and they sometimes seek to dissimulate their own expressions – handy when it comes to preventing others from stealing a good feeding spot, for instance. More often they may play their own expressions to the hilt to get something they want, sometimes using 'social staring' to supplant others from feeding spots. Interestingly, among gorillas it is the subordinates who use this technique, often quite successfully, whereas among chimpanzees it is the dominants, more testimony to the gorillas' gentle nature.

Left: this mother's expression reflects the happy demeanour of the group overall. Below, a gorilla splashes playfully.

A silverback has it made. Life revolves around him. Because food is abundant, there is no need for territorial scuffles with other groups, indeed no need for territories, and home ranges of different groups overlap. This leaves time to lounge as harem females wrangle over who gets to groom him, and progeny of all ages spill about him at play. When it is time to forage, he gives himself priority access to the most convenient feeding spots. Despite appearances, this is well-earned. It is he who decides when, where and how fast to move camp,

A poised silverback need only frown to end a squabble

The gorilla is a veritable *pater familias* among apes. His intrinsic power and authority seem sufficient to hold the fort forever, but 35 years is generally the limit.

pacing the day's travel to accommodate the sick or injured. A poised, well-respected silverback need only frown to end a squabble between females or to quiet rumbustious youngsters. And especially, in the event of an attack by leopard, human or lone marauding silverback, he is there to defend his family. Though a power-packed chest beating or charging display is usually enough to dissuade an aggressor, a silverback will fight to the death if he must. Gorilla groups usually average between five and ten members but can reach 30, and exceptionally up to 60. With gorillas stretching from western swamps, where the sweltering heat stifles, to eastern Afromontane forest where the damp chill creeps into your bones, it is easy to imagine

how habitat plays its part in determining group size. Because gorillas dislike competition, the general rule is the larger the foraging patches the greater the group size. It is therefore not surprising that the larger groups are found among the almost exclusively herbivorous Eastern species, particularly in the Mountain Gorillas; one group hovers around 60. Further west, fruit in season is abundant, but it tends to grow in clumps. Too large a group of the more frugivorous Western Lowland Gorillas might cause tension over who gets access to the patchy resources. Where large groups do exist, they may spread out over ½ km to forage or split into smaller groups for the day, meeting up again to nest together in the evening. Here groups consist of a dominant silverback, three or four females and four or five young. Judging from nest counts in the hills, the elusive Western Cross River Gorillas appear to have the smallest groups of all. Beyond food resources, group size may also be determined by female

When a female transfers from her natal group, she has left her family behind to form a new one. Though her interactions will be cordial enough, she will rarely groom or bond with the unrelated females in her new group, reserving her affections for her young and her silverback.

preference. In the wild, before a female reproduces for the first time, usually at around the age of eight, she is most likely to transfer from the group where she was born to another. She may transfer to a large existing group, but if she does, she will rank low in the hierarchy, peaceable

High-ranking females have better access to the silverback

As with all great apes, gorilla reproduction is slow, with the interval between infants four years and infant mortality high. In the course of her lifetime, up to 40 or 50 years, a mother will usually raise two to six offspring.

as it may be. She would prefer to join a strapping, lone silverback with a prominent head crest and pronounced saddle, one who will be only too glad to start his own harem where, first come first served, she will be number one. She may alternatively decide to join a newly-formed group where it is better to be number two than number twelve. Most often, she will transfer at least once more in her lifetime, either because she is disillusioned with her new silverback, or because after years with the same group, something has upset the status quo and it is time to move on. Seeking a high ranking place in the hierarchy has nothing to do with ego. Its benefits are down-to-earth. Firstly, an established hierarchy where everyone knows their place means less energy is wasted on disputing resources. In the case of gorillas, for whom food is generally plentiful, the issue is one of reproductive resources, that is of the opposite sex. High-ranking females have better access to the silverback, hence

better protection from predators and abductors, both for themselves and for their young. This is important because unprotected nursing mothers are at high risk of losing their infants to outside males who, through infanticide, hasten a female's return to oestrus, improving their own likelihood of luring her away in the near future. After all, a mother who discovers that the silverback on whom she has depended is unable to defend her offspring might decide she will have better reproductive success next time under the protection of the stronger male. Infanticide is widespread among the Virunga Mountain Gorillas, where it accounts for 37 per cent of infant mortality. Females here often choose another strategy, such as joining a large group, but one with more than a single silverback. The more silverbacks there are to defend the group, the less risk there is of mothers losing their babies. Once it was thought there was only one silverback to a group, but gorillas are constantly confounding their observers and it appears now that some groups have two or more fully grown males, usually but not always father and son(s) or brothers. Among Mountain Gorillas, as many as 40 per cent of groups are 'multi-male', and it may be due to pressure from the females. Normally, no dominant silverback would welcome other males who sooner or later are likely to challenge his authority, split off with part of his harem, or mate surreptitiously with his wives (genetic studies

of multi-male groups show that 15 per cent of infants can be attributed to the second-in-command). Since a dominant silverback may seek to dissuade reproductive females from transferring out but will not prevent them, if he wants to hang on to his harem and peace of mind, he may learn to accept, tolerate and even cooperate with other adult males in his group. But there is never any guarantee. At present, after decades of stability, researchers and rangers are having a hard time keeping up with the sweeping changes underway in some of the best known groups in the Virungas. Groups are breaking up, males are running off with females, females are transferring, males are taking control and losing control, things that didn't happen in the past when the overall population was smaller.

"Mountain Gorilla group behaviour is stable insomuch as generally one silverback in association with other adult males still maintains group cohesion and defence. However, extremely interesting dynamics have set in recently among some of the 'original' groups, Beetsmee's, Shinda's and Pablo's, that have been monitored since Dian Fossey's time by Volcano National Park researchers, rangers and guards. Sometimes there are six, sometimes fewer. Shinda's group in particular was always known for its large number of silverbacks, which was considered important for the group's cohesion. We hope that continued observation of these groups will lead us to an explanation of these occurrences."
Fidèle Ruzigandekwe, *Director of Conservation, Office of Tourism and National Parks*

Gorillas are born, usually at night, after an 8½ month gestation period. Weighing a mere 2 kg, they are almost totally helpless. They can, however, cling to their mother's front with their hands and, to a lesser extent, their feet.

By three months of age,
infants begin to walk,
ride on their mother's
back and explore their
environment. The white
tuft of fur on their
bottom at this age is
the gorilla equivalent of
our 'baby on board' sign.

Almost more surprising is the fluidity with which it is happening. Where it will all lead remains to be seen. Multi-male groups are uncommon in Western Lowland Gorillas, but so is the violence between different groups and between groups and solitary males that typifies their highland cousins. The peaceful encounter between neighbouring Western Lowland silverbacks has been one of the major surprises to come from the growing body of research on this subspecies in recent years. Baffled scientists have turned to genetics in search of an explanation. Most of the males ranging in the site studied are related. They may be father and son or they may be brothers but, in all cases, they appear to form dispersed networks of male kin.

Like females, males of all gorilla subspecies emigrate, though rather than join another group they usually remain alone or associate with other bachelors until they have become silverbacks in their own right, usually at around 11 to 13 years of age. At this point they are ready to found a group for themselves by luring away females, taking over a 'widowed' group or, in Eastern Gorillas, ousting another silverback. But most encounters between Western Lowland Gorillas appear to be friendly because most of them are silverback family reunions. Paternal analysis of Western Lowland Gorilla groups, virtually all of which count only one silverback, indicate that all offspring are sired by that silverback, with no evidence that females are having

trysts with outside males. Males can be
fairly certain that they are related, and
certainly while growing up they remain long
enough in each others' company, usually
for about eight years, to bond and be able
to recognize each other in later years.
The fact that Western Lowland Gorillas
might find benefit from paternal kin biased
behaviours, even outside their immediate
groups, may be a feature common to all
African apes and humans. The genetic
evidence, however, remains to be confirmed
by behavioural observation in the field.
Once a female has found a mate who
suits her, it is time to start her own family.
Almost all mating is at her invitation.
Dian Fossey described her behaviour
as "outlandishly coquettish" while the male's

Gorillas have been observed mating face to face

is "pretentiously blasé". She sidles up to him,
slightly turned away, and waits for a signal,
sometimes for up to 15 minutes. When one
comes, she will usually turn and back up
to 'present' to him. Most mating takes
place with the silverback sitting or standing
behind her, hands on her waist, as she
braces herself on her hands or elbows,
although Western Lowland Gorillas have
been observed mating face to face.
Copulation generally lasts one to two
minutes though sometimes longer, and
is repeated throughout the female's
two-day period of oestrus.

Both male and female appear concentrated,
the silverback with pursed lips, the female
with hers compressed. The female is more
vocal than the male. She whimpers,
he gives a shuddering rumble which has
been dubbed 'the train grunt'. This attracts
the attention of other young males and

During the first six months, baby gorillas develop about twice as fast as humans. Though juveniles express a particular interest in the infant at this stage, the little one rarely strays far from its mother's side.

Female gorillas reproduce for the first time between the ages of nine and twelve years. They remain fertile until the end of their lives.

outside silverbacks. It is when females are cycling that the most clashes occur, putting the dominant male in a very foul mood. Perhaps there is a reason behind his aloofness. The tiny, helpless infant comes into the world after a period of gestation lasting just less than our own. In the following months, its mother will stay close to the silverback. The baby itself will spend its first weeks clinging to its mother, as best and as close to her milk-swollen breasts as it can. At two months, an infant may start attempting to crawl and even begins to grin and chuckle. At three months, it begins to walk and climb on and around its mother. Interestingly, this is the only time a mother may positively encourage an activity in her infant. The infant, on the other hand, is extremely interested in what its mother is doing, often attempting to imitate her and finding ways to engage her in play or get her to share food. In other primates, sharing foods with infants is both a way to supplement their diets and to teach them what they can and cannot eat. Among gorillas sharing is always at the youngster's instigation, as when an infant tries to take food away from its mother. This works about half the time as long as her child is still a baby, but sometimes the mother is the one to take food away, and as the baby grows and learns which plants and parts it can eat and how to process them, the food sharing ends. What is interesting here is how, in contrast to the mother's seeming indifference to her infant's education, the infant itself actively creates opportunities to acquire knowledge and skills. Weaning takes place at about 2½ years. As gorillas grow, play takes on increasing importance. Play is where well-rounded gorillas learn the motor and social skills that will carry them through the rest of their lives. They may start by playing alone, bouncing, hanging or running around in ways that one day could come in handy in the face of predators or aggressors. Once mastered,

this type of play tends to fall off after the first two years. After the few months of never breaking contact with their mother, for the next three years, with gradually increasing confidence, gorillas spend some time alone exploring and handling objects, but also engage increasingly in social forms of play and display. Social play tends to reflect the roles that each will assume as an adult. Male infants will grow up to take on a peripheral role in the defence of the group before spending time alone or in a bachelor group. As might be expected, they tend to play more often and more roughly than females, and prefer other males as playmates. However because male-female relationships will also be such

Play tends to reflect the roles that each will assume as an adult

a major part of their lives, males also play with females, always reciprocating when females are the instigators. Because the social focus of females in adulthood will be the silverback, females too prefer to play with male playmates rather than with other females. They often remain friends with their male playmates into adulthood. By playing with males, females may learn their ways and better negotiate life in the harem later on. Both sexes combine their games with play faces, play bites, and play displays such as chest beating and clapping or drumming

the ground or other surface to get attention, much like chimpanzees. The capacity to recognize their playmates' subtle cues of intention in complex games of tag, chasing and wrestling, and ability to distinguish between real and made-up situations reveals cognitive capabilities that will serve them their whole lives through.

The capacity to recognize playmates' subtle cues will serve them their whole lives

Though adult females and juveniles often play with youngsters, the youngsters' own preference goes to peers. Unlike some primates, notably baboons and humans, mother gorillas seldom meddle in their offspring's choice of game, or of playmate.

It matters little whether we consider gorillas and the other great apes 'people' like early Western observers did, or whether we adopt today's view that humans are in fact great apes. Anyone can intuit our closeness in their eyes, in their expressions, in their gestures.

We share almost 99 per cent of our genes with chimpanzees and bonobos, our closest living relatives. Gorillas are a close second. That human beings are different from apes is obvious. Pinpointing why is not so easy. In the centuries since the apes were first discovered, philosophers, biologists, anthropologists and cognitive scientists have run the gamut in search of what would draw the definitive line, and in so doing have often blurred it further, particularly where the issues of cognition and consciousness are concerned. A paradigm shift is underway, leading away from the Cartesian Man-mind / animal-machine dichotomy that has dominated academic thinking in the West. Up to now, as Martin Schönfeld writes: "Studying the affinities of humans and animals would appear to violate this well-established rule, and would risk sliding down the slippery slope from fawns to Bambi, from rabbits to Thumper, from science to myth." But as the results from worldwide field and laboratory research in different areas converge, it appears increasingly that cognition and consciousness belong to a sort of dynamic continuum, where both similarities and differences have something to teach us. Picasso owned a painting by a chimpanzee named Congo. He is not the only one. 'Ape art', as it is called, holds tremendous appeal for humans. It feels right. Dr. Anne Zeller wanted to find out why. She analyzed 396 colour drawings done by captive chimpanzees, orangutans, gorillas and young children, identifying regularities which ruled out the possibility that they were mere scribbles. Some of the features were common across the board for all species: four was the number of colours most often used; blue was the most frequently used colour overall. Yellow ranked fourth, yet all four species preferred to start a picture with yellow (except human females, who chose green first, yellow second). Other regularities were species and/or gender specific: chimpanzees consistently ran off the edge of the paper, human girls did so least, human boys ran off more than orangutans. Humans tended

Cognition and consciousness belong to a dynamic continuum

to use a wider and more flexible range of colours and more zigzags. As for gorillas, they used diagonal lines much less often than the others, but used arcs and open roving lines more. They used more smears and left much less of the paper free of colour, but when they ran off the page, it was generally only toward themselves. They used much more red and males were the only ones to top their pictures off with a dash of purple, whether it was among their initial colours or they mixed it themselves. Gorillas also painted more spots, a common feature of prehistoric art. No doubt Sir Julian Huxley, the British biologist and one of the founders of UNESCO, was right to ponder the origins of human art when in 1942 he observed a gorilla at the London zoo thoughtfully

Der junge Gorilla im Aquarium zu Berlin. Originalzeichnung von G. Mützel.

"King is an older animal who was born in captivity and who has a strong rapport with his keeper/ trainer. The thing that was really interesting is that when she would say to him "draw a rainbow" or "a flower" or "a gorilla" or something, the things that came back – while you wouldn't call them representational – the rainbows had a mixture of colours in a horizontal sweep, the flower paintings were kind of puffy and pink and green. When asked to do a gorilla he used black, and people he used pink (we were all Caucasian). There was a definite difference between the blotchy pictures and horizontal pictures and his choice of colours made sense."
Dr. Anne Zeller, *professor of anthropology, Waterloo University, Canada*

trace his shadow on the wall. Three times. Did the London Zoo gorilla know the shadow was his own? Ever since Gordon Gallup Jr. developed the mirror self-recognition test in 1970, it has served as the best way to measure self-awareness such as our own in other animals. The method involves marking a spot on some part of an animal where it can only be seen in a mirror. If, looking in a mirror, the animal reacts to the spot, by touching its forehead, for example, it is considered to demonstrate knowledge of itself. Apes, elephants and dolphins score positive. Dogs and cats do not. Nor do human infants of 18 months and under. Nor do many gorillas, at least not for the most part. This may be due to the fact they have an aversion to eye contact. They would first have to overcome their own gaze, then that of the test's observers. Many experiments have been conducted to over- come this reluctance, using angled mirrors, for instance, or habituating a gorilla to use mirrors to other ends before attempting the mark test. The results are mixed, although gorillas seeing themselves on CCTV screens

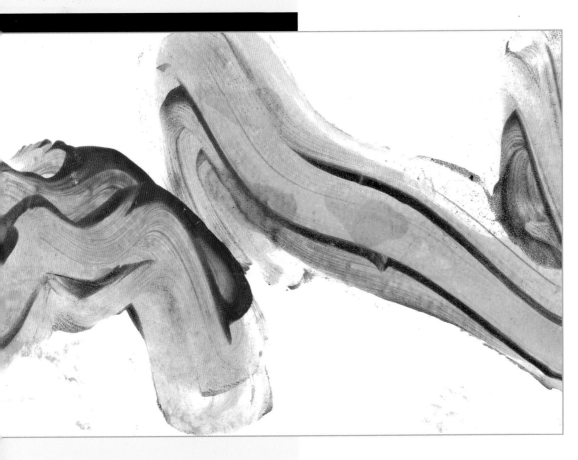

Left: In 1883, the Berlin
Aquarium acquired
an infant gorilla (notice
the white rump tuft).
Raised in many respects
as a human child, it
survived only 18 months.
Right: A rainbow painted
by the gorilla King at
Monkey Jungle, Florida.

have shown self-directed behaviour. The most success has been with gorillas who are already highly accustomed to humans and their rude stares and who have lost their natural 'gaze aversion'. Perhaps it is best with gorillas to look at unprompted behaviour for signs of self awareness. One such example is that of seven-year-old Zura, a female Western Lowland Gorilla observed by J. Tanner and R. Byrne at the San Francisco Zoo. Unlike humans, apes have little control over their facial expressions. For instance, when play is in the air, it is hard to hide it. So when the need arose to keep a straight face, Zura found her way around her natural inability. She covered her face with her hands. This was always when she was at play with her pal Zubie. When she did, play was delayed. Sometimes she did so when she wanted to pounce on him unsuspectedly. Sometimes it was to avoid resuming rough and tumble play when she was still tempted but had had enough. Once was when an older, respected gorilla entered their play space and play was not appropriate. Zura only covered her face when Zubie could see her. She was aware that her own facial expressions were giving her away and what would follow if she didn't conceal it. She was aware. Zura was also being funny. Humour researchers say that incongruity is a basic building block of humour. For an event to be perceived as incongruous, the person – or gorilla – has to have a memory of what the normal event is like, and it can only be appreciated if the individual is in a playful state of mind and realizes that there is a paradox. In a verbal joke there is always a paradox. In play, asking a partner through body language and other signals to believe an attack is not real is a form of paradox. A playful ambush is a simple punchline. Koko is one of only two Western Lowland Gorillas to have been taught sign language, at which she is extraordinarily proficient, combining signs to make phrases, but also inventing signs themselves. She uses her ability to finish off pranks. Once she tied Dr. Penny Patterson's shoelaces together and gleefully signed "Chase". Other times she would find a way to get her gorilla friend Michael into trouble and then with a smile, a chuckle and a sign of the hand call him "Stinker". A charming way indeed to disarm critics who like F. M. Müller in 1871 wrote, "The one great barrier between brute and man is language… Language is our Rubicon, and no brute will dare cross it." Unlike Müller, whom a colleague once referred to as 'the humbug of the century', Koko knows how

Humour may play an important role in gorilla society

to crack a joke. Her level of humour concurs with other assessments of gorilla cognition as equivalent to that of a six-year old human child. Grown gorillas are nevertheless adults in their own right and not children, and humour may play an important role in gorilla society as a whole. It most likely helps them – as it does us – to bond and therefore to cement existing social relationships and ease into new ones. And they appear to know what they are doing. One area that was long considered the private domain of humans

Behavioural observations in the wild, cognitive experiments in captivity and genetic analysis in the laboratory all attest to the veracity of our kinship. Here, a gorilla contemplates its reflection.

is tool use. Given the evidence, tool use was extended to the great apes, to the exclusion of the gorilla who, it was speculated, had lost the skill somewhere along the evolutionary trail. As it became increasingly clear that tools, not to mention mirrors, are used by a great many other animals, gorillas began to lose cognitive face. Gorilla defenders

graciously pointed out that they didn't need tools. Mountain Gorillas demonstrate amazing skill at getting into defended fruit, for instance. But Western Gorillas don't even need to. Why bother with hammers and anvils or stripping twigs of leaves to fish for termites when with your powerful jaws you can crack an oil nut with your teeth and with

your mighty fists bust open a termite hill at one stroke? And yet for years captive gorillas had spontaneously used tools in zoos and animal parks, using sticks to obtain out-of-reach food or other objects of interest, throwing sticks and wood at humans or other gorillas, even using coconut fibres as sponges and logs as ladders. Had they really lost what it takes to handle a tool? Then one day in October 2004, gorilla history was made in Congo. Thomas Breuer was watching Western Lowland Gorillas at Mbeli Bai from an observation platform. There was Leah, a female gorilla from a group that had been observed for almost ten years, but whose group had not visited the clearing for six months. During their absence, elephants had created a new pool. Leah stood gazing into the unfamiliar pool for a minute before wading in on two feet. After only a few steps,

Above left: A young gorilla still wearing a 'playface' after a rough and tumble game of chase. Above right: A human observer respecting the gorilla social code of 'gaze aversion'.

she was waist deep. Returning to her point of entry, she broke off a branch that was sticking out of the water and tested its depth in front of her. Then she waded out another 8 to 10 m., using the branch to test the water and as a walking stick for support. The scene was interrupted when her infant began to cry and she returned to shore, leaving the stick behind. Six weeks later Efi, a female from another group, broke off the trunk of a dead shrub and pushed it into the ground to use as a stabiliser; she hung on to it with one hand as she pulled up aquatic herbs with the other. She then placed the same trunk on the soggy ground and crossed over it on two feet. Wet footprints had been observed on trunks elsewhere. Was this more common than had been thought? Did the Lowland Gorillas come up with similar solutions to similar problems

"I think therefore I am."
Are gorillas challenging
Descartes on his own
terms?

Sticks and stones. Since 2004, a series of observations of female gorillas in particular have overturned decades of thinking about gorilla tool use in the wild.

in a similar environment on their own or did they learn it somewhere? Hundreds of miles away at Kagwene Mountain in Cameroon, in the course of a three-year study of Cross River Gorillas, these rarest of the gorillas were observed on three occasions throwing clumps of grass and once a stick at – or back at – humans. The last time was in response to a man who had thrown rocks at them.

Did the Cross River Gorillas learn it recently from humans or have they been doing it since Hanno the Navigator's day? Are these different populations demonstrating cultural diversity? In the meantime, Itebero, a 2½ year old gorilla confiscated from poachers the year before, surprised her keepers at a sanctuary when she began smashing palm nuts between rocks; a far more sophisticated demonstration of tool use than throwing clumps of grass. Furthermore, she was doing it with remarkable dexterity, whereas it takes most chimpanzees years of learning to refine their technique. Yet she had no one to imitate. This sudden reversal in our knowledge about gorillas raises as many questions as it answers. One thing is certain. It stresses the importance of supporting long term research if we are to gain better understanding of and respect for our cousins and, no doubt, ourselves.

REASON TO HOPE

In July 2007, photographs of dead Mountain
Gorillas carried by mourning villagers hit
the cover page of newspapers worldwide.
It was a shocking image. The gorillas, from
Virunga National Park in the DRC, had been
shot at point blank range, execution style,
and apparently left as a warning to those
who would thwart illegal charcoal activities
in the park. It was a shocking story.
But it also drew international attention
to the plight of the gorillas as little had
in the past. And the timing was uncanny.
Gorillas have never been more at risk.
By chance, at the very same time as the
killings, the ten gorilla countries were planning
a meeting under the United Nations
Convention on Migratory Species, to be held
in Paris just months later to negotiate
the terms of a first-of-a-kind treaty to protect

The Congo basin
accounts for close
to one-fourth of the
world's moist tropical
forest, second only
in surface area to the
Amazon. An estimated
50 per cent is under
logging concessions.

all gorillas, across all borders. Habitat loss due to forest clearance for food crops and, to a lesser extent, logging were once the greatest threats and already local conservationists and international organisations had their hands full battling to secure the gorillas' future. Today's threats are far faster moving. Chief amongst them are the bushmeat trade and ebola haemorrhagic fever. Although it is impossible to know exactly how many gorillas have been killed by either means – dead gorillas tell no tales – we do have figures for some populations. Ebola is a contagious, incurable disease that kills about 80 per cent of infected humans, slightly fewer chimpanzees,

While surprisingly Western Lowland Gorillas appear to prefer secondary forest, clear cut forests do not necessarily grow back. Here erosion has washed away the soil that would have sustained, if not forest, then at least crops or pasture.

and a whopping 95 to 99 per cent of gorillas. In the light of available evidence, it is estimated that one-quarter of the world's gorillas may have succumbed to the disease since 2000. If we search for the positive side, ebola rightly strikes fear into would-be gorilla meat traders, particularly when governments issue edicts about the dangers of eating ape meat in an ebola-afflicted area, effectively halting hunting, at least for a time. Initially, ebola spreads to humans through contact with contaminated meat – from

the killing, butchering or eating of infected primates. But in a strange twist, ape-to-ape contagion hits hardest where they are at least risk of encountering poachers. This is because the otherwise healthy populations are more dense there. In the past, the surviving 5 per cent of ebola-decimated populations might have been able to rebound, meeting up with other survivors and distant groups, and gradually building up their numbers again, despite their slow birth rate. With today's fragmented habitat, gorillas

With today's fragmented habitat, gorillas are less resilient

are less resilient and all the more susceptible to other pressing threats. In addition, ebola has the potential to destroy years of eco-tourism investment. To take just one example, the gorillas at the Lossi Gorilla Sanctuary in northwest Congo, whose habituation was so hard-earned, were wiped out by the disease, along with ecotourism revenues for the local people. For now, only Western Lowland Gorillas have been hit, but outbreaks among humans have occurred in Uganda and the DRC, raising fears it may spread to the Mountain Gorillas, whose entire population is confined to two small areas. The effect would be devastating. A vaccine does now exist and despite the cost and the difficulty involved in distributing it to the all-the-more sparse groups that would require it, experts are looking at possibly rolling out a major vaccination scheme along the leading edge of the spreading ebola epidemic.

The bushmeat trade is more insidious. Local populations have always hunted wild animals to supplement their own diets with proteins from the forest. But with the boom in commercial logging and mining, commercial hunting has reached new levels. Indeed, since the 1990s logging has led to a mind-boggling rate of deforestation, particularly in West Africa. This is not just reducing ape habitat. All those hardworking loggers in the concession towns must be fed, and the logging roads themselves have provided convenient access for a new breed of hunters, armed with modern shotguns and traps to meet the demand. It was easy money compared with the lot of loggers in the forest and the jobless in the cities. As more hunters joined the ranks they organised a way to deal with the 'surplus' bushmeat they were bringing in.

Right: One of ten of the habituated Eastern Lowland Gorillas in the Kahuzi-Biega National Park have lost a hand or foot to snares left out to trap the forest's hoofed animals.
Far right: Rangers on patrol in the Virungas.

Truckloads of wild animals of every variety now roll toward the cities where a taste for the delicacy of wild animal meat, endangered or otherwise, has developed. In some areas, gorillas are a part of the take. A thousand miles to the east, civil war in the DRC sent droves of both refugees and rebels into the forest, rendering law enforcement nearly impossible. One of the reasons for the civil war was to gain control of the many precious resources the area boasts. The lawless mining of coltan, the metal ore used in cell phones and portable computers, and the hunters who provided food for the miners, impacted on the endemic

Fortunately, gorillas are not to the taste of everyone

Eastern Lowland Gorillas. So when in 2004, tensions eased and conservationists began to assess the damage, they estimated that only 5,000 remained. That was a staggering 70 per cent fall from the previous census, taken in 1994, which estimated the population at around 17,000. Each time the political situation begins to stabilise, the timber companies move in, compounding the problem. Fortunately, gorillas are not to the taste of everyone. To those living near the Cross River Gorillas of Kangwene, gorillas are people, which may explain why they were so dedicated to the creation of the Kangwene Gorilla Sanctuary. Mountain Gorillas too are mostly exempt from the bushmeat trade, though there have been

We are beginning to understand just how much the African forest on which the livelihoods of so many people depend, indeed on which our very atmosphere depends, relies in turn on the gorillas and the other unwitting keepers of this ecosystem.

some casualties due to refugees from the civil war and cross-border skirmishes that have strained the region since the early 1990s. Astonishingly, thanks to the dedicated efforts of rangers and support from several charities, their numbers actually increased by 17 per cent during this same period. Wildlife tourism is certainly one of the major solutions. In 2006 the illegal charcoal trade in Goma, much of it from the Virunga National Park, was estimated at $30 million. Tourism there earned less than $300,000. But tourism in the DRC is down for the very reason that trade in illegal charcoal is up: civil war. Uganda provides the perfect counter-example. At $30 million in revenues from well-managed parks, hotels and services, Uganda's wildlife tourist infrastructure rivals the DRC's illegal charcoal trade.

The difference is that this is in foreign exchange earnings and about 70,000 jobs have been created in Uganda. Tourists spend $4.7 million a year on chimpanzee and Mountain Gorilla viewing permits alone, revenues that have benefited the surrounding communities in the form of health and community centres, schools, roads, mills etc. Uganda is even bolstering the rest of its tourist offerings, restoring its kingdoms' landmarks and proposing lakeside resorts

Left: Bushmeat for sale by the roadside.
Top: Animal parts with purported medicinal properties. Below: In the DRC, illegal charcoal sells at $25 a sack. Refugees and locals alike use it for fuel and to filter water.

In 2008, thanks to decades of ongoing efforts, and despite their small numbers, Mountain Gorillas are the least threatened of any gorilla at present. Rwanda, Uganda and the DRC have nevertheless agreed to a cross-border plan to strengthen park security to safeguard the species, and their rangers, 110 of whom have lost their lives in the DRC trying to protect their wards.

and mountaineering facilities.

The case of Uganda shows that, with proper management, the direct and indirect impact of gorilla tourism can be far reaching. The challenge now is to develop it in other areas of Africa. Without exception, the involvement of and benefit to local populations is prerequisite to success, and many efforts focus on sustainable development of this kind. Sometimes grassroots organisations provide the impetus. In 1992, an experiment in the habituation of Western

Sometimes grassroots organisations provide the impetus

Lowland Gorillas was undertaken in the Lossi forest by Congo's Ministry of Forestry and by Forest Ecosystems in Central Africa (ECOFAC). It was novel both in its participatory approach and in the fact that the area involved was not already part of a protected zone. Aware of the possible community spin-offs, the local population became involved from the start. The pilot project lasted three years, after which the villagers themselves, convinced of its potential, addressed a request to the Ministry that the area be classified as a sanctuary, agreeing to relinquish highly valued ancestral lands. The process, which would take five years, involved creating an association of the beneficiaries, determining the statutes and rules that would govern the association on the one hand and the sanctuary on the other, and training to ensure effective collective management of the natural resources. In 2001 the Lossi Gorilla Sanctuary was officially decreed by government. Though it is still recovering from the loss of its gorillas due to ebola, the story of the Lossi Gorilla Sanctuary stands as a positive example of grassroots initiatives. One of the most unlikely places to look for hope is the climate crisis. Increasingly, corporations and other institutions or individuals in the developed world are willing to reduce their carbon dioxide (CO_2)

Tourists keep a respectful distance to avoid spreading germs to gorillas. Even a common cold can be dangerous to these creatures who are susceptible to human infections ranging from the chicken pox to tuberculosis, but have built up no defence against them.

emissions, but have not the financial or technological resources available to overhaul their infrastructure in the immediate future. Financial mechanisms offer a way for companies to 'offset' their emissions by reducing carbon dioxide in other ways. Oceans, soil and forests serve as carbon sinks, removing CO_2 from the air. Since every tree planted in the tropics absorbs about 23 kg of CO_2 from the atmosphere per year, financial institutions are now looking at forests and reforestation as possible investment opportunities. The issue here is to be sure they do not lose sight of the forest for the trees.

"One of the big questions at the moment is the role of forests as carbon sinks, the role of forests in mitigating climate change. Potentially, it can achieve a lot of the things we all want to achieve because for the first time the City, the stock market, is looking at investing serious money in the carbon market. That is likely to result in investment in forest management in a way which keeps the forest as a functioning ecosystem. GRASP is involved in this and we are trying to remind people that forests are not just trees, and to work with people who are going to be affected so they understand what's expected of them and what's likely to happen."
Ian Redmond *OBE, Chief Consultant UNEP/UNESCO-GRASP (Great Apes Survival Partnership), Founder Ape Alliance*

Forests are complex systems. Plants and trees and the animals that eat the fruits that carry their seed have evolved together, becoming co-dependent. We have seen the example of the gorillas from West Africa's

Here at an Aspinall Foundation sanctuary, orphans of the bushmeat trade are being primed for release in a location where they can be closely monitored and range freely without competition or conflict from their more forest-savvy wild cousins.

swampy lowlands who keep their heart healthy by consuming grains of paradise and whose digestive system in turn enables germination. So too, the whole of the forest depends on relationships of this kind.

In the words of Ian Redmond, "The health of the planet depends on the tropical forests, and the health of the forests depends on the primates, elephants and birds that sow the next generation of trees." Gorillas are fully protected in all ten countries where they are found, but enforcement is conditional upon financial and political stability, a sound legal framework and effective cross-border cooperation. Indeed, gorilla ground was broken on these latter two issues when on 1 June 2008 the Agreement for the Conservation of Gorillas and their Habitats came into effect. The Gorilla Agreement legally binds the countries that sign it to respect its terms. While these are adapted to the specific context of each signatory state, the focus is always on identifying gorilla habitats and ensuring their protection and

management, working together to maintain a network of suitable habitats, and working together to eliminate poaching, particularly in the areas along state boundaries. Unlike the Kinshasha Declaration, which set the same goals for all great apes in 2005, the Gorilla Agreement is a legally binding treaty. The governments that sign are committing themselves to introduce legislation to enforce it, and they are agreeing to be held accountable for it. For a long time to come, the fate of the gorillas, like that of the forests, will depend on a combination of investment and know-how by international institutions and non-governmental organisations; the commitment and the stability of national and local governments; and the consent and involvement of local people and of grassroot initiatives. In them we place our hope.

The gruelling albeit rewarding work of habituating Western Lowland Gorillas is beginning to pay off. From observation platforms, researchers and visitors alike can at last observe the gorillas rooting out swamp herbs and, with any luck, testing the water's depth with a stick.

Recommended reading

- De la Bédoyère, Camilla and Bob Campbell (2005) No One Loved Gorillas More: Dian Fossey - Letters from the Mist. Palazzo Editions.
- De Waal, Frans (2005) Our Inner Ape: the Best and Worst of Human Nature. Granta Books.
- Fossey, Dian (1983) Gorillas in the Mist. Hodder & Stoughton.
- Parker, Sue Taylor, Robert W. Mitchell and H. Lyn Miles, eds. (1999) The Mentalities of Gorillas and Orangutans: Comparative Perspectives. Cambridge University Press.
- Redmond, Ian; forward by Jane Goodall (2008) The Primate Family Tree: the Amazing Diversity of our Closest Relatives. Firefly Books. (If purchased at www.4apes.com, a share of the proceeds will benefit Ape Alliance)
- Redmond, Ian (1995) Eyewitness Gorilla and other Primates. Dorling Kindersley.
- Ruoso, Cyril and Emmanuelle Grundmann (2007) The Great Apes. Evans Mitchell Books.
- Russon, Anne E. and David Begun, eds. (2004) Evolution of Thought: Evolutionary Origins of Great Ape Intelligence. Cambridge University Press.
- Schaller, George B. (1964) The Year of the Gorilla. University of Chicago Press.
- Taylor, Andrea B. and Michele L. Goldsmith, eds. (2003) Gorilla Biology: A Multidisciplinary Perspective. Cambridge University Press.

Further information

The following organizations are dedicated to the conservation and welfare of gorillas and suggest concrete ways to contribute.

Ape Alliance – a collective lobby to be reckoned with, which develops position papers on key issues and serves as a hub of information for member groups. www.4apes.com

Aspinall Foundation – manages two gorilla rescue and rehabilitation projects in Africa, contributing to conservation in the areas where it is active. www.totallywild.net/jaf

Berggorilla – this organisation publishes the Gorilla Journal (accessible on-line), providing some of the most comprehensive, readable material available. www.berggorilla.org/english

Dian Fossey Gorilla Fund International – protects gorillas through regular monitoring and works with local communities to boost education and reduce poaching and encroachment. www.gorillafund.org

Great Apes Survival Project (GRASP) – a UNESCO/UNEP partnership launched to tackle the immediate threat of ape extinction. It focuses on international dialogue and policy, conservation initiatives, technical and scientific support to governments where gorillas range, field projects and fund and awareness raising. www.unep.org/GRASP/

Gorilla Organization – fosters a grass-roots approach to conservation by promoting sustainable livelihoods and empowering local people to deal with threats to gorillas. Organizes gorilla runs. www.gorillas.org

Wildlife Conservation Society (WCS) – has worked to protect all species of gorillas for fifty years. Dr. George Schaller is Vice President. www.wcs.org

Acknowledgements

Martin wishes to thank warmly: Michèle Depraz
of WWF International, for helping him to gain access
to both the Mountain Gorilla project in the DRC
and to the various bushmeat monitoring projects
in Central Africa; Apenheul Primate Park, Netherlands,
for allowing him to photograph at their zoo; Amos
Courage of the John Aspinall Foundation for granting
access to the foundation's gorilla projects in
the Lesio-Louna Reserve (Congo) and La Mpassa
reserve (Gabon); and the numerous and very
dedicated staff of all of the projects who allowed
him to accompany them and provided a place to stay.

Letitia extends her gratitude to: Ian Redmond
of Ape Alliance in the UK for his vast knowledge
of apes and their conservation and his highly pertinent
amendments; Bob Campbell in Kenya for sharing
his experience on habituating the mountain gorillas,
his photo of Dian Fossey and his gentle voice that
soothes the soul of a writer on a deadline;
Dr. Anne Zeller of Waterloo University in Canada
for discussing her fascinating articles on ape art
and for the painting by King; Fidèle Ruzigandekwe,
Director of Conservation at the Office of Tourism
and National Parks in Rwanda for outlining
the changes under way in the Volcano National Park
Mountain Gorilla group; Dr. Donato Bergandi
of the Muséum national d'Histoire naturelle, Paris
for his epistemological critique and suggestions
for the chapter 'Next of Kin'; Sabrina Krief
of the Muséum national d'Histoire naturelle, Paris
for contact information; Abigail Girling of the Gorilla
Organization for contact information and the photo
of the gorilla run; John Mitchell of Evans Mitchell
Books and Christine Baillet of Empreinte & Territoires
for their patience; Bruno her husband for his support;
and Tosca, her whiskered research assistant
for bringing her rubber bands and nesting
on the desk like a pint-sized Cross River Gorilla.

OTHER

 Wild things...

TITLES

Wild Things...
Creatures of the Deep Blue
ISBN: 978-1-901268-31-7

Wild Things...
The Great Apes
ISBN: 978-1-901268-31-7

Wild Things...
Tiger – The Lord of the Jungle
ISBN: 978-1-901268-40-9

Other wildlife titles published by

 **Evans Mitchell Books**

www.embooks.co.uk

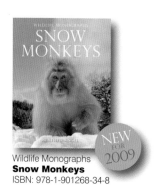

Wildlife Monographs
Snow Monkeys
ISBN: 978-1-901268-34-8

Wildlife Monographs
Living Dinosaurs
ISBN: 978-1-901268-36-2

Wildlife Monographs
Giant Pandas
ISBN: 978-1-901268-13-3

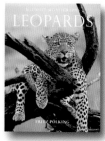

Wildlife Monographs
Loepards
ISBN: 978-1-901268-12-6

Wildlife Monographs
Sharks
ISBN: 978-1-901268-11-9

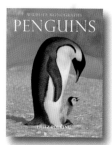

Wildlife Monographs
Penguins
ISBN: 978-1-901268-14-0

Wildlife Monographs
Polar Bears
ISBN: 978-1-901268-15-7

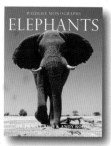

Wildlife Monographs
Elephants
ISBN: 978-1-901268-08-9

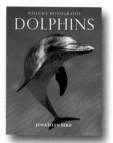

Wildlife Monographs
Dolphins
ISBN: 978-1-901268-17-1

Wildlife Monographs
Wolves
ISBN: 978-1-901268-18-8

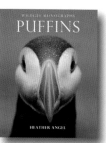

Wildlife Monographs
Puffins
ISBN: 978-1-901268-19-5

Wildlife Monographs
Monkeys of the Amazon
ISBN: 978-1-901268-10-2

Wildlife Monographs
Cheetahs
ISBN: 978-1-901268-09-6